Happy
Eid al Fitr
The sweet festival

WAYLAND

Lexile: _____

AR/BL: _____

AR Points: _____

Published in paperback 2017 by Wayland
© Hodder and Stoughton 2017

Written by Joyce Bentley

Editor: Corinne Lucas
Designer: Ariadne Ward

A catalogue for this title is
available from the British Library

ISBN: 978 1 5263 0128 4

10 9 8 7 6 5 4 3 2 1

Wayland
An imprint of
Hachette Children's Books
Part of Hodder & Stoughton
Carmelite House
50 Victoria Embankment
London, EC4Y 0DZ

An Hachette UK Company
www.hachette.co.uk
www.hachettechildrens.co.uk

Printed in China

Picture credits: Cover image © Samere Fahim Photography; p4 © Murat Taner/
Corbis; p5 © FADEL SENNA/Stringer; p6 © OZAN KOSE/Stringer; p7 © MADAREE
TOHLALA/Stringer; p8 © ALI HAIDER/epa/Corbis; p9 © Ali Haider/epa/REX/
Shutterstock; p10 MOHAMMED HUWAIS/Stringer; p10–11 © Muhammad Mostafigur
Rahman/Demotix/Corbis; p12–13 © Kami/arabianEye/Corbis; p13 © nisargmedia.
com/Shutterstock.com; p14 © kiraziku2u/Shutterstock, Inc; p15 © Rich-Joseph
Facun/arabianEye/Corbis; p16 © Pacific Press/Contributor; p17 © Samere Fahim
Photography; p18 © A katz/Shutterstock, Inc; p19 © Dan Kitwood/Staff;
p20 © John Mulligan/Ocean/Corbis

Background images and other graphic elements courtesy of Shutterstock.com.

Contents

What is Islam? 4

Holy Ramadan 6

What is Eid al Fitr? 8

Getting Ready for Eid 10

Praying Together 12

Eat, Eat, Eat! 14

Children Love Eid 16

Family Fun 18

Thinking About Eid 20

Eid Greetings Card 22

Glossary and Index 24

What is Islam?

Islam is the name of the religion that *Muslims* follow. It began around 1,400 years ago when the *Prophet Muhammad* ﷺ was visited by the Angel Jibril who brought him messages from *Allah* (God). These words were later written down and became the *Qur'an*.

The Five Pillars of Islam teach Muslims the set of rules that Allah wants them to live by.

The Five Pillars of Islam

1 Believe in only one God, Allah (shahadah)

2 Pray five times a day (salah)

3 Give money and food to charity (zakah)

4 Fast during *Ramadan* (sawm)

5 Make a *pilgrimage* to Makkah (hajj)

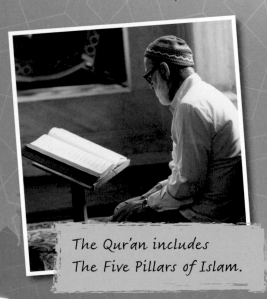

The Qur'an includes The Five Pillars of Islam.

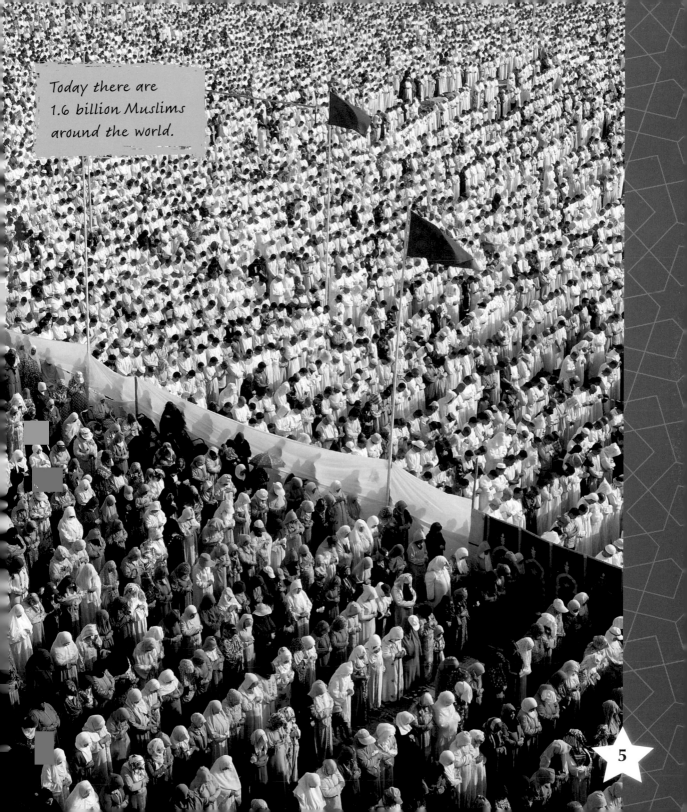

Today there are
1.6 billion Muslims
around the world.

5

Holy Ramadan

Every year Muslims *fast* during the ninth month of the Islamic calendar, known as Ramadan. They do not eat or drink during daylight hours for 29 or 30 days.

Iftar is the family meal eaten by Muslims after sunset during Ramadan.

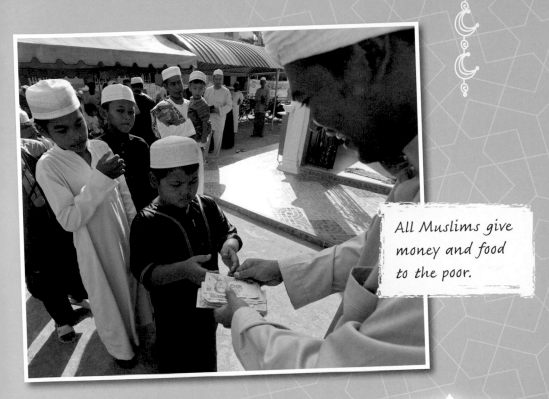

All Muslims give money and food to the poor.

Fasting is difficult to do but it reminds Muslims of the suffering of the poor and what it is like to live without food. Some people, including the old and sick, do not have to fast.

"We fast to show we are thankful for what we have."

What is Eid al Fitr?

Eid al Fitr is a festival that marks the end of Ramadan. Muslims around the world stop fasting and feast for up to three days. It is a time of celebration, joy and thankfulness.

People shop after sunset to prepare for the Eid al Fitr holiday.

Eid al Fitr, also known as Eid, begins when the new moon is seen in the night sky.

Pronunciation Guide:
Eid al Fitr
eed al fitter

The new moon appears over a mosque in United Arab Emirates.

Getting Ready for Eid

Eid is a very exciting time. Houses are cleaned, greetings cards are sent and the cooking begins. Later, families and friends come together for a great feast.

Muslims take great pride in looking their best. Many people buy new clothes, shoes and jewellery for the festival.

During Eid, girls often decorate their hands with mehndi (henna).

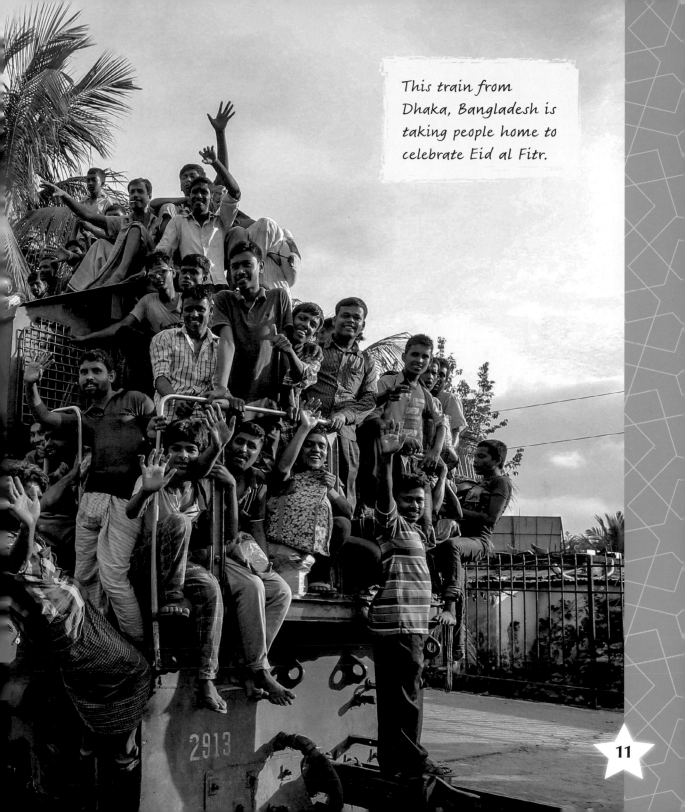

This train from Dhaka, Bangladesh is taking people home to celebrate Eid al Fitr.

Praying Together

On the morning of Eid, people get up early to go to the mosque. Everyone washes their hands and face, and removes their shoes before entering the mosque.

A large group of men praying in a mosque in Abu Dhabi.

An *Imam* leads the prayers. Muslims pray five times a day to remember the importance of Allah. They thank God for giving them the strength to fast during Ramadan.

After prayers people gather to wish each other Happy Eid!

13

Eat, Eat, Eat!

Muslims all over the world celebrate Eid al Fitr by feasting on their favourite foods. To break the fast a small, sweet breakfast is eaten. After prayers several dishes are served from fish and meat curries, salads and breads to sugary puddings and cakes.

Children celebrating the end of Ramadan.

During Eid, people visit their relatives to wish them 'Eid Mubarak'. They are given something to eat at each house as part of the celebration.

'Eid Mubarak' is a common greeting that means happy or blessed Eid.

عيد مبارك

In Arabic

A Muslim family eat an Eid meal together.

Children Love Eid

Eid is a special time for children. During Ramadan older children fast from the age of about 11. Young children show their love and loyalty to Allah by giving up their favourite foods.

Once the Eid morning prayers are over, children rush to find their friends. Sweets are the most popular treat to enjoy during Eid al Fitr. Now they can eat as many sweets as they like!

A group of children meet up after morning prayers in Allahabad, India.

DID YOU KNOW?

Eid al Fitr is often called The Festival of Sugar or The Sweet Festival

Sweets are everywhere during Eid, including baklava. A puff pastry and almond sweet.

17

Family Fun

After the feast many families go out. In some countries there are fairs and parades to enjoy. Dancers perform in traditional costume and there is live music.

Traditional dancers perform during Eid.

People enjoying a ride on bumper car during Eid celebrations in London.

Over Eid festival there are special events for children and trips to the amusement park or beach. Many countries hold craft markets and sell food. Days often end with a dramatic firework display.

Thinking About Eid

Eid is a special time for Muslims as they come together to celebrate their faith. They show love for each other and feel joy at their love for Allah.

Eid al Fitr is a happy time. How would you feel being part of the festival?

Sunset signals the end of the first day of the Eid al Fitr celebrations.

Word clouds

You can make your own word cloud. First, think of some words to describe Eid al Fitr. Draw a shape or picture, such as a moon, and fill it with your words.

An Eid word cloud

pray peace
sacrifice eid zakat festival
allah celebrate family qur'an
ramadan muslim month
mubarak strength tradition
mosque holy fasting

Can you think of any other words to describe Eid?

21

Eid Greetings Card

Many people send greeting cards for Eid al Fitr to celebrate this special festival. Try making one of your own.

Materials
You can use card, coloured paper, tissue paper, felt-tip pens, scissors, glue, paint, ribbon, jewels and decorative tape.

Your card
To start, take a piece of A4 card and fold it in half, width ways. Draw images that reminds you of Eid al Fitr on coloured paper. Try drawing a mosque, a star and crescent moon, candles, fireworks, trees, flowers, or Islamic patterns. Ask an adult to help you cut them out and glue them to your card. Stick on any jewels or decorations you have.

The crescent moon and star reminds people that Eid al Fitr has begun.

22

You could decorate your card with traditional patterns from Islam, such as these ones. Try copying or tracing them.

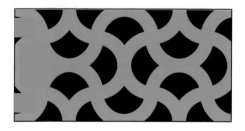

Greetings

Write 'Eid Mubarak' on your card to wish people a blessed Eid al Fitr.

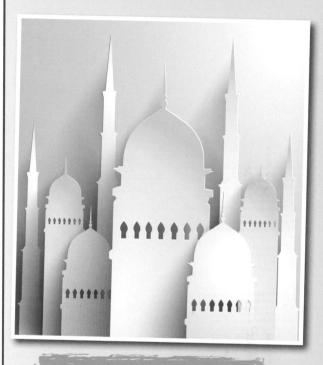

Why not cut out an outline of a mosque in white paper to place over a pattern.

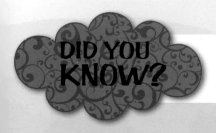

DID YOU KNOW?

It is forbidden in Islam to draw any people, animals or birds.

Glossary

Allah – the name Muslims give God

Fast – to not eat for a period of time

Iftar – the meal eaten after sunset during Ramadan

Imam – a Muslim leader

Islam – the Muslim religion

Mehndi – a temporary tattoo worn at times of celebration

Mosque – the Muslim place of worship

Muhammad ﷺ – prophet and founder of Islam

Muslim – a follower of Islam

Pilgrimage – a journey to a special place

Prophet – people chosen by Allah (God) to be his messengers

Qur'an – the sacred book of Islam containing the words of Allah

Ramadan – the ninth month of the lunar Islamic calendar, when Muslims fast

Index

Allah 4, 7, 13, 16, 20, 21

Eid al Fitr 8, 9, 10, 11, 12, 13, 14, 15, 16, 17, 18, 19, 20, 21, 22

family 6, 10, 14, 15, 18, 21
fast 6, 10, 14, 15, 18, 21
festival 8, 10, 16, 20, 21, 22
food 4, 7, 14, 16, 19

greetings card 10, 22

Islam 4, 6, 22, 23

money 4, 7
mosque 8, 12, 21, 22, 23
Muslim 4, 5, 6, 7, 8, 10, 13, 14, 20, 21

pray 2, 4, 7, 12, 13, 14, 16

Qur'an 4, 21

Ramadan 4, 6, 8, 13, 16, 21

sweets 16, 17